My Friend Has Down Syndrome

by Amanda Doering Tourville   illustrated by Kristin Sorra

Thanks to our advisers for their expertise, research, and advice:

Dianne McBrien, M.D.
Clinical Associate Professor of Neurology, Development & Behavior
University of Iowa Children's Hospital

Terry Flaherty, Ph.D., Professor of English
Minnesota State University, Mankato

PICTURE WINDOW BOOKS
a capstone imprint

Editor: Jill Kalz
Designer: Nathan Gassman
Production Specialist: Jane Klenk
The illustrations in this book were created with mixed media - digital.

Picture Window Books
1710 Roe Crest Drive
North Mankato, MN 56003
877-845-8392
www.capstonepub.com

All books published by Picture Window Books
are manufactured with paper containing at least
10 percent post-consumer waste.

Library of Congress Cataloging-in-Publication Data
Tourville, Amanda Doering, 1980–
My friend has down syndrome / by Amanda Doering Tourville ; illustrated by
Kristin Sorra.
p. cm. — (Friends with disabilities)
Summary: "Explains some of the challenges and rewards of having a friend with
Down Syndrome using everyday kid-friendly examples."—Publisher provided.
Includes index.
ISBN 978-1-4048-5751-3 (library binding)
ISBN 978-1-4048-6110-7 (paperback)
1. Down syndrome—Juvenile literature. I. Sorra, Kristin, ill. II. Title.
RC571.T738 2010
618.92'858842—dc22   2009035268

Printed in the United States of America in North Mankato, Minnesota.
092011
006365R

My name is Carmen. This is my friend Sarah. Sarah and I met at school, but we're also in the same dance class. Sarah has Down syndrome.

Sarah is a lot of fun to be around. She's one of the most cheerful people I know. I like telling Sarah jokes. Her laugh sounds like a honking goose!

4

DID YOU KNOW? Down syndrome is a condition some babies are born with. It affects people of all races, rich and poor. No one knows why it happens. There is no way to prevent it.

Sarah looks a little different from other kids.
But we all look different from each other, right?
Life would be boring if we were all the same.

#1 fri

DID YOU KNOW? Kids with Down syndrome tend to be short. Their eyes look smaller and slant upward. However, not everyone with Down syndrome looks exactly alike.

Sometimes other kids
make fun of Sarah.

That makes me mad. It's never
OK to make fun of someone.

I didn't know any other girls my age who wore glasses before I met Sarah. Now I'm not alone! Sarah and I like to trade glasses so we can see how funny the world looks.

Sarah and I love ballet. We dance in the "Nutcracker" every December. Sarah wants to be a sugar plum fairy this year. I want to be a mouse.

DID YOU KNOW? Kids with Down syndrome enjoy all the same things other kids do. They enjoy sports, movies, music, and hanging out with friends.

Sarah needs extra help at school. She goes to special math and reading classes. The teachers work one-on-one with her.

DID YOU KNOW? Kids with Down syndrome have learning disabilities. They learn more slowly than other kids their age.

I miss Sarah when she's not in school. She goes to the doctor a lot. Sometimes she gets scared.

DID YOU KNOW? Kids with Down syndrome often have other health problems. About half of all people with Down syndrome have heart problems. They may also have hearing or vision problems.

I cheer up Sarah when she's feeling sad. She does the same for me. She might draw me a picture or lend me her favorite bracelet.

Sarah wants to work in a children's hospital when she gets older. She likes to help people. I know she'll be great at it.

DID YOU KNOW?
Many adults with Down syndrome have jobs, in all sorts of areas.

Maybe she'll let me run
the x-ray machine!

I like being friends with Sarah. She's cool.
Sarah always knows how to make me smile!

What Is Down Syndrome?

Down syndrome is a condition some babies are born with. It affects how a child's body and mind grow. Down syndrome is caused by cells that split, or divide, the wrong way. Cells are the tiny building blocks of which all life is made. There is no cure for Down syndrome. Kids with Down syndrome look different than other kids. They usually have flatter faces, eyes that slant upward, and small ears. They also have medical problems, such as heart or stomach troubles. Kids with Down syndrome grow slower than other kids their age. They also learn slower. Therapy can help them learn to walk, talk, and do other important life skills better. Many kids with Down syndrome grow up to have jobs in all sorts of areas, including business, medicine, and the arts. Some even go to college.

Glossary

condition—an illness

learning disability—a condition that keeps a person from learning information the way most people do

prevent—to keep something from happening

therapy—treatment for an injury or physical or mental problem

To Learn More

More Books to Read

Glatzer, Jenna. *Taking Down Syndrome to School.* Plainview, N.Y.: JayJo Books, 2002.

Moore-Mallinos, Jennifer. *My Friend Has Down Syndrome.* Hauppauge, N.Y.: Barrons Educational Series, Inc., 2008.

Plucker, Sheri. *Me, Hailey.* Hollidaysburg, Penn.: Jason and Nordic Publishers, 2005.

Internet Sites

FactHound offers a safe, fun way to find Internet sites related to this book. All of the sites on FactHound have been researched by our staff.

Here's all you do:

Visit *www.facthound.com*

FactHound will fetch the best sites for you!

Index

Look for all of the books in the Friends with Disabilities series:

My Friend Has ADHD

My Friend Has Autism

My Friend Has Down Syndrome

My Friend Has Dyslexia